Tom Wolfe Carves Fancy Canes

Tom Wolfe

Text written with and photography
by Molly Higgins

4880 Lower Valley Road, Atglen, PA 19310 USA

Contents

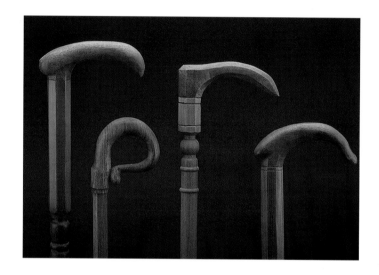

Designed by John P. Cheek
Type set in Seagull Hv BT/Souvenir Lt BT

ISBN: 0-7643-1343-6
Printed in China

Published by Schiffer Publishing Ltd.
4880 Lower Valley Road
Atglen, PA 19310
Phone: (610) 593-1777; Fax: (610) 593-2002
E-mail: Schifferbk@aol.com
Please visit our web site catalog at
www.schifferbooks.com or write for a free catalog.

We are always looking for authors to write books on
new and related subjects. If you have an idea for a
book, please contact us at the above address.

This book may be purchased from the publisher.
Please include $3.95 for shipping.

In Europe, Schiffer books are distributed by
Bushwood Books
6 Marksbury Ave.
Kew Gardens
Surrey TW9 4JF England
Phone: 44 (0)20-8392-8585
Fax: 44 (0)20-8392-9876
E-mail: Bushwd@aol.com
Free postage in the UK. Europe: Air mail at cost.
Please try your bookstore first.

Introduction

The cane is a simple accessory with a lot of personality. Some are sleek and elegant, others are twisted and gnarled, others are bright and silly. Some hide flasks, or even knives! Like a hat or tie, a cane is an expressive part of any ensemble. What better way is there to show off your individuality than with a cane you've carved yourself?

In addition to the endless creative potential they hold, there are many practical reasons that canes make great carving projects. They are small enough that you can produce a beautiful handle design with a relatively small time investment, and they are good pieces to practice on. They make terrific gifts, and they are always top sellers at shows.

It has never been easier to carve your own canes. In years past, you would have to use a lathe or take the time to carve a stick. Now, home improvement centers, hardware stores, and other builder supply sources carry a wonderful variety of turned spindles for beds, stairways, and tables that are also perfect for canes.

In this book, we will be carving an especially functional cane handle—one that doubles as a nutcracker. Once you understand its basic construction, you will probably come up with many of your own designs. The gallery that follows has dozens more ideas to get your imagination fired up. So sharpen that knife and get busy!

The Carving Process

Bed and stair spindles are excellent for canes. Some table legs are good too, although they can be a little heavy. These spindles come in a whole array of woods, including maple, cherry, and oak. Poplar is nice and lightweight. Some come with screws in the end, some have dowels, and some will require you to fit them to the handle yourself. One way or the other, the handle should be secured on the end of the spindle with some kind of pin for strength. Make sure you shop around to see the variety of shapes and sizes that are out there!

Whatever the spindle has on the end, you're going to have to make the block fit onto it.

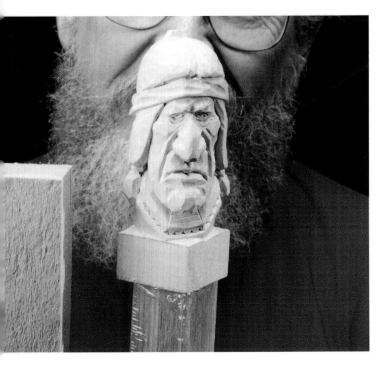

It should be a good, snug fit, like this.

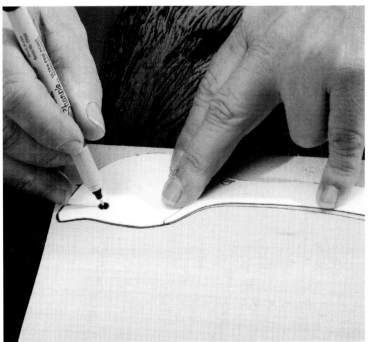

Make sure you mark the spot for the dowel well. I'm going to use a 1/4-inch dowel, but you can also use a bigger one. For harder woods you can get away with using a smaller dowel, but softer woods like this basswood should have a 1/4- to 3/8-inch dowel. Remember, it has to be strong enough to crack nuts with!

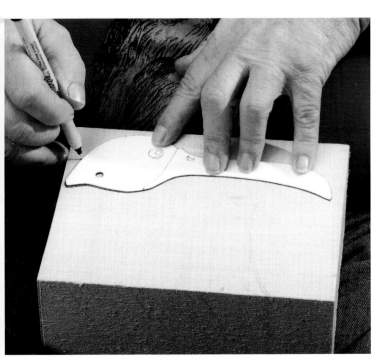

Here is the pattern for a nut-cracking gooney bird. I'm using a pen to mark the wood only because it shows up better in the photograph. It's better to use a pencil, because then there's no threat of the ink running when you paint or shellac the piece.

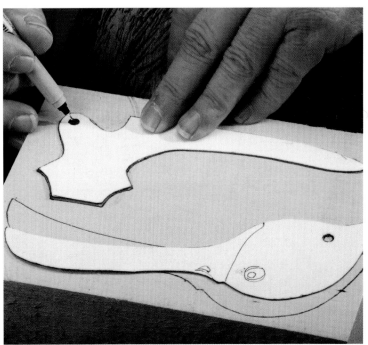

Trace and mark the pattern for the jaw.

Then cut out what you've traced using a bandsaw. I usually use four-inch stock, and I've cut this one down to two inches because that's all we need.

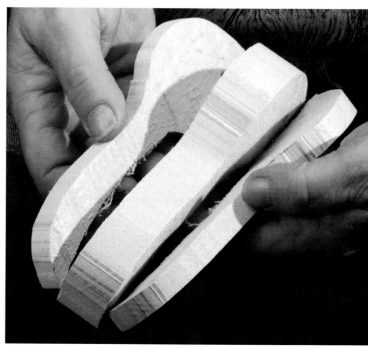

I made the cuts with the bandsaw. Make sure that center piece is at least an inch thick, to fit a pecan.

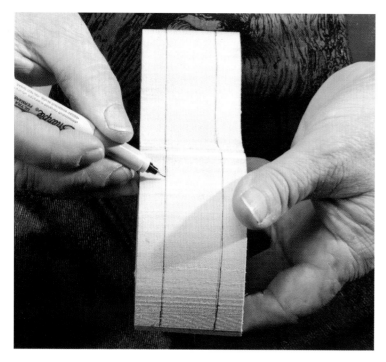

Then, mark it to cut another half inch off of either side with the bandsaw.

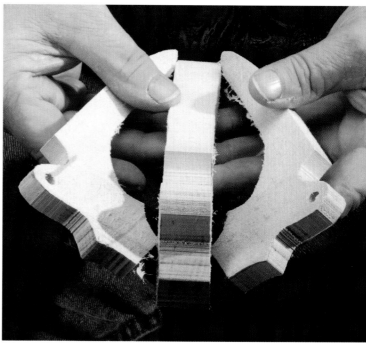

The jaw piece needs to be cut the same way.

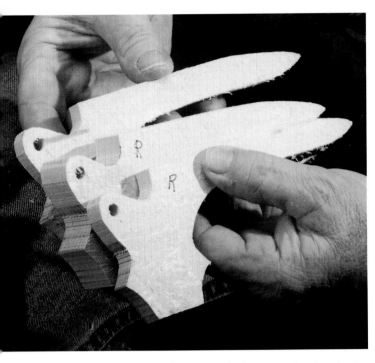

Mark the pieces left and right, so you don't get confused and cut two of the same side. When you go to glue them back together, the saw marks will fit.

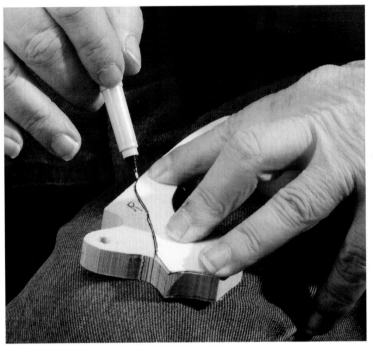

Marking the other side.

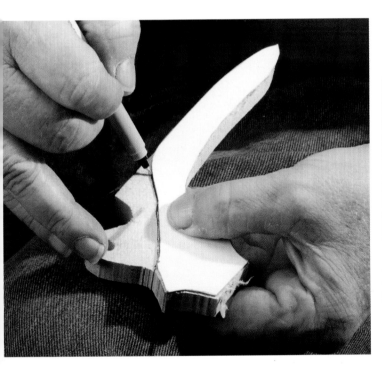

We're going to saw off the inside parts of the outside pieces. Use this pattern to mark before you cut.

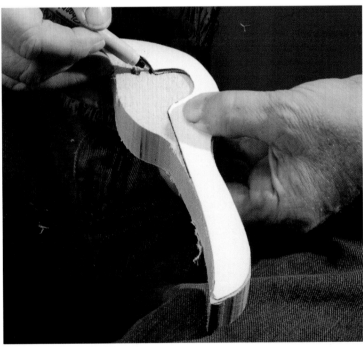

Mark the center piece for cutting using this pattern. Since I'm using the bandsaw to cut away the excess, I'm only marking one side. If I were carving it out, I'd mark both.

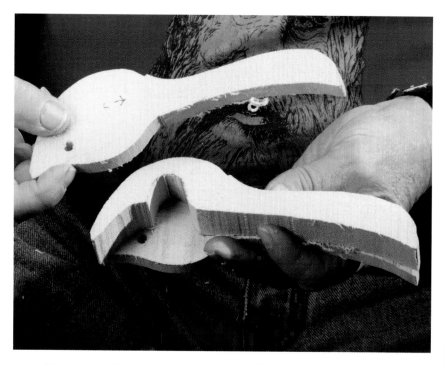

Here is what the head pieces should look like after you cut them.

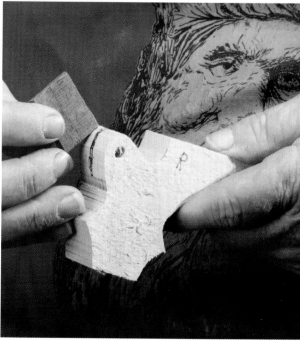

Since I'm using basswood, which is pretty soft, I want to strengthen the jaw piece a little by making a spline out of a little bit of hardwood, like this walnut here. Make sure the grain on the hardwood is running up and down; that's where its strength comes from. First mark where the spline will go. Then slice it out with the bandsaw.

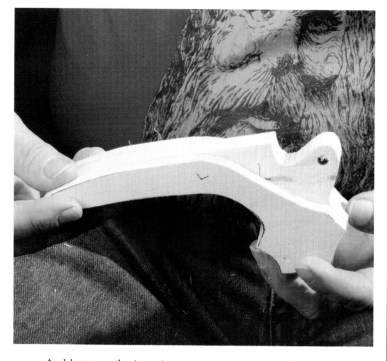

And here are the jaw pieces.

Cut the slot only wide enough for the piece of hardwood to fit snugly into it, making sure the grain is going up and down like this. Then glue it in place and trim away the excess.

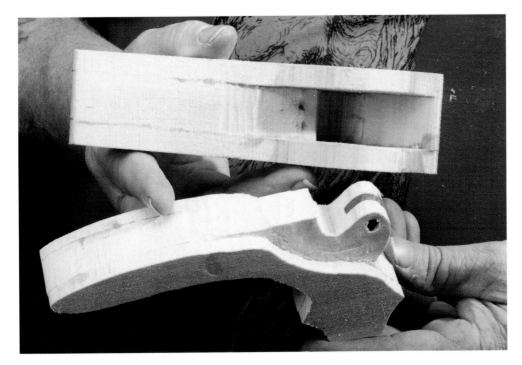

Now you can glue all sides together to look like this. Make sure you apply some pressure while it's drying, using a clamp or something similar. It will take overnight for it to fully bond, but it should be ready for carving in about an hour and half.

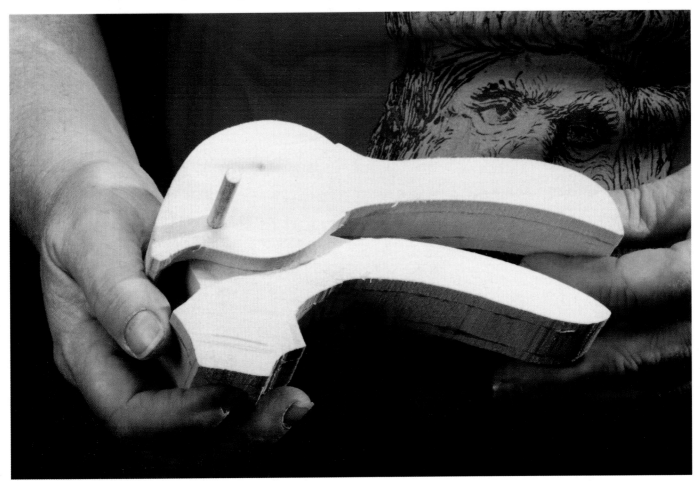

Fit the two pieces together, and try and work the pin through it.

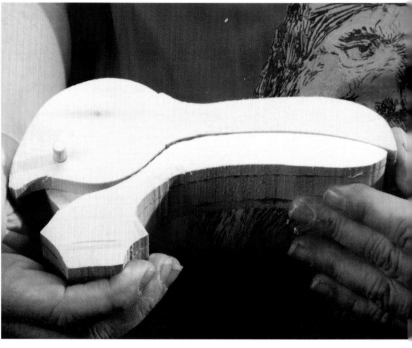

You might need to make some small adjustments to make the pieces fit. For instance, I'm going to have to take a little off right here.

Now they fit a little better. A good way to test it is to snap the jaw on its hinge against the head part. You should hear wood on wood, hitting evenly.

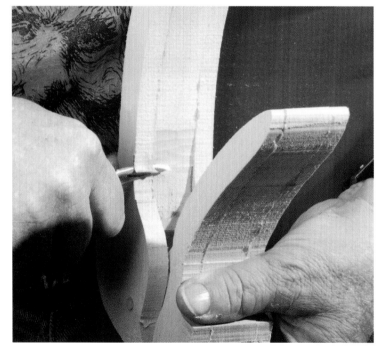

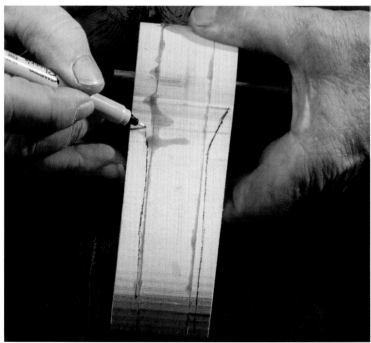

Don't cut too much away.

Now I want to take a little more away from the sides (with the bandsaw) to narrow the beak, which is also the cane handle.

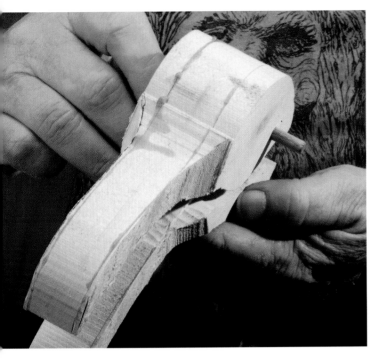

Try to avoid cutting as far in as the glue joint, but if you do, that's alright.

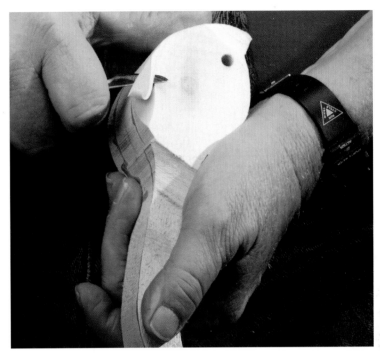

Then, knock the corners off all the way around.

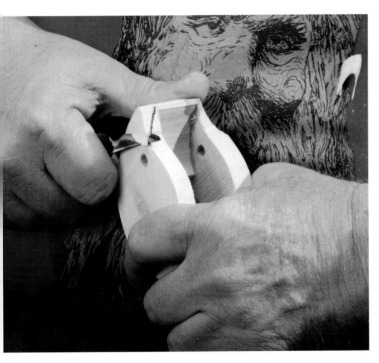

Now we're ready to carve. I'll start by narrowing this area down like I've marked, but be careful you don't cut too much away.

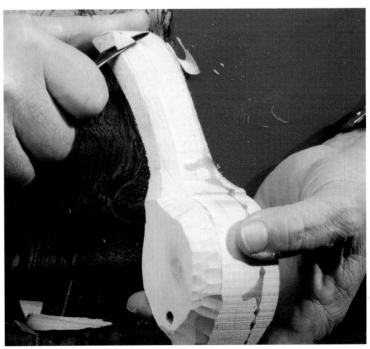

Progress.

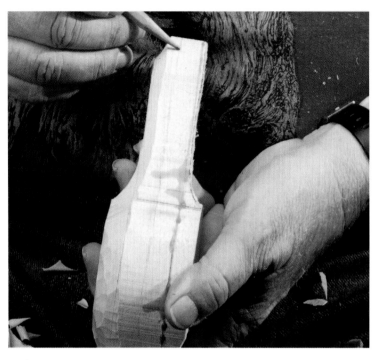

I forgot to mark my center line! It's important you always have a center line so you cut the same amount off of both sides.

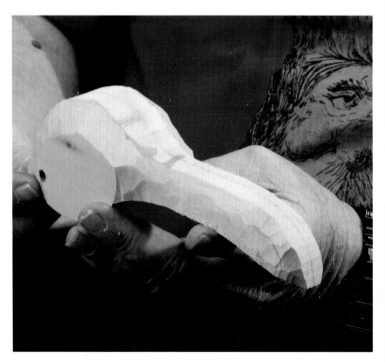

Now that the corners are gone, I'll go back over the piece to get rid of roughness, glue marks, and saw marks.

Hold the knife like this and pull toward yourself to get the long smoothing motion.

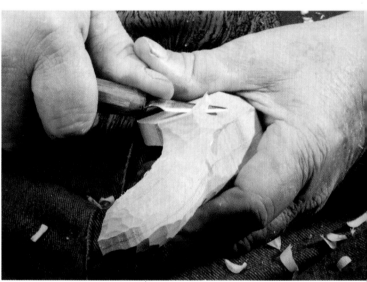

Another good way to cut is by rocking the knife back and forth on your thumbs in a fulcrum-like motion. I use these two cuts about 90% of the time.

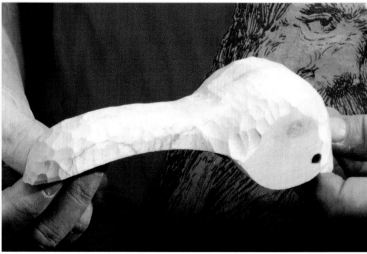

Progress.

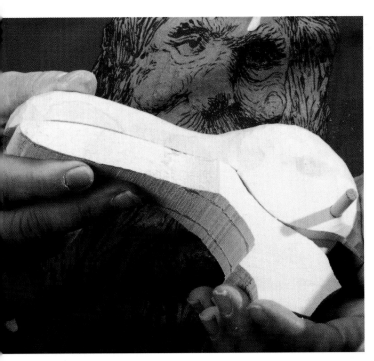

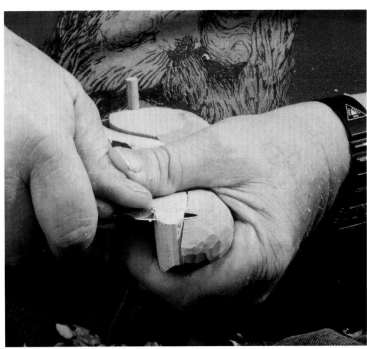

Then carefully carve away the excess.

Keep fitting the jaw part back in to make sure it still fits.

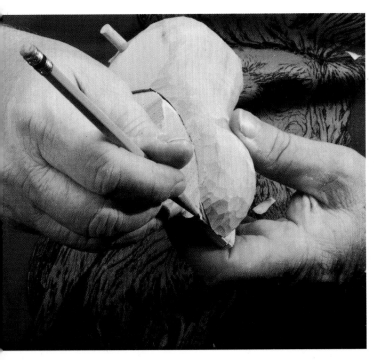

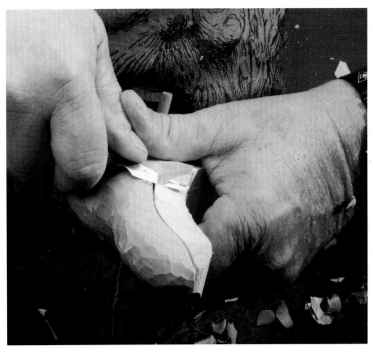

Make sure the beak lines up all the way around.

Using the head piece as a guide, mark the jaw piece so that it matches the upper part of the beak.

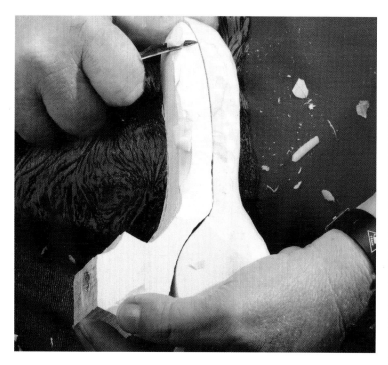

Now knock the corners off of the jaw piece.

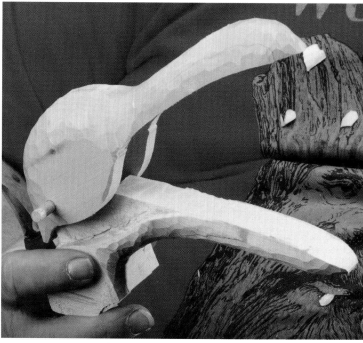

He's already begging for a pecan! Focus on the head itself, and not on the base where it will attach to the cane. Also, before you get into any of the details, make sure you get all of the lumps in the right place, whether they're for eyes, ears, or a nose.

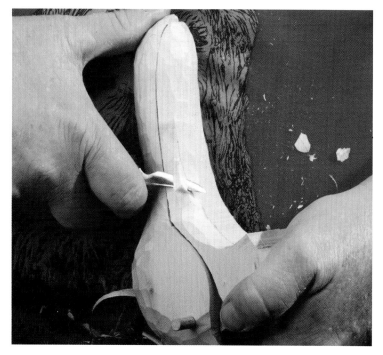

Carve it so that the beak tapers nicely, but don't take away too much.

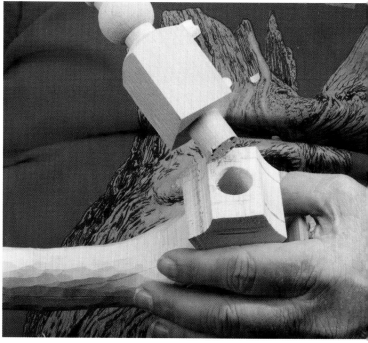

Drill the hole in the base to fit the dowel on the spindle snugly.

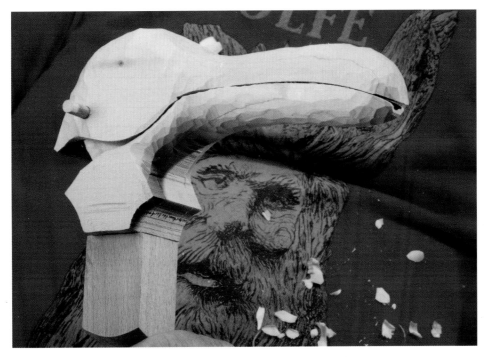

You can see that the base of the handle is a little big for the spindle. We're going to have to carve a little off of each side so that it fits evenly against the sides of the spindle.

 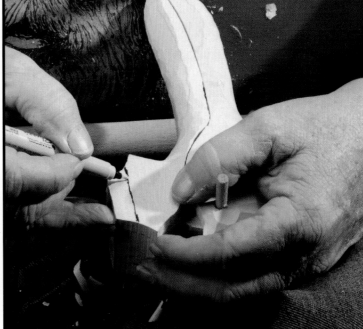

Use the spindle to mark what needs to be cut away.

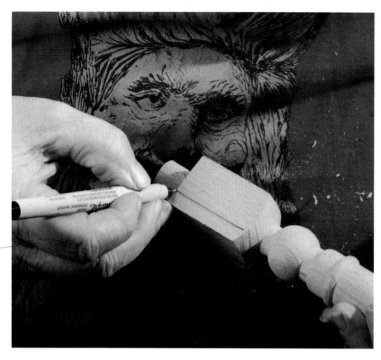

I also want to cut the corners off of the spindle, so I'll mark it like this.

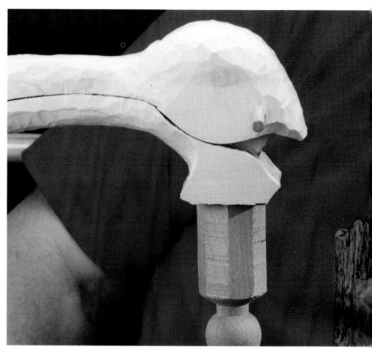

Using the bandsaw, I also cut off the corners on the spindle to look like this.

Using the bandsaw, I cut away part of the base to fit like this. You might need to drill the hole for the dowel a little deeper.

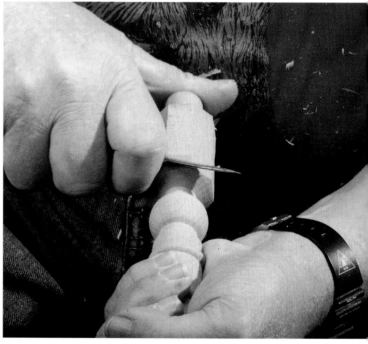

Smooth out the saw marks on the spindle. A pocket knife is good for carving harder woods, like the oak that this spindle is made of. Sometimes I leave the chip marks on every other side to add a little texture. You could also sand all the sides smooth if you'd like.

Keep in mind that all the spindles out there are not made perfectly; sometimes they have warps. Fit the handle on it and turn it so that the spindle is aligned with the body. If there's a warp, make sure it faces front and not out to either side. Then mark which side is the front of the cane, which actually is the back of the head on the handle.

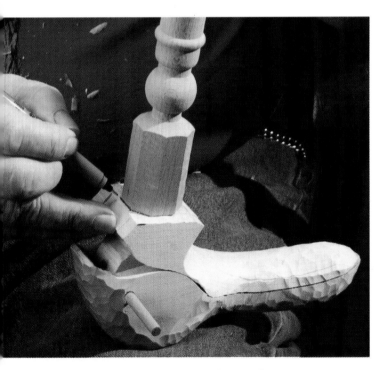

I made the cuts for the octagon on the spindle using my eye, so it's not going to be perfect. Trace the octagon onto the base of the handle so you know how far in to cut.

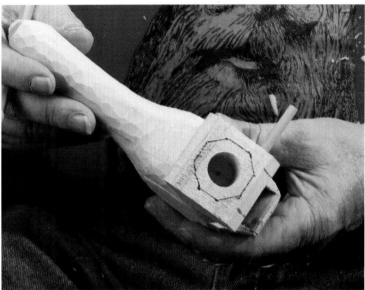

It should look like this.

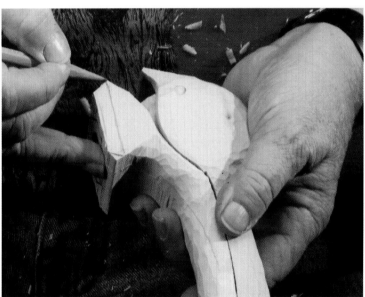

I'm marking a line where the feather texture will stop, to create a sort of base where the cane attaches to the spindle.

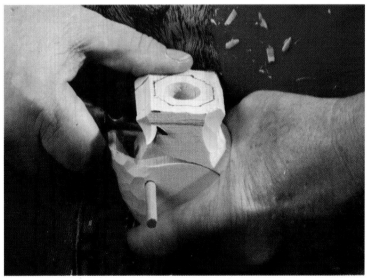

Cut wood away so that the base is an octagon shape.

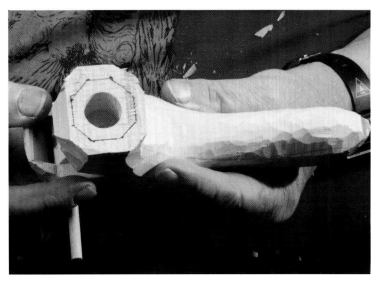

Progress.

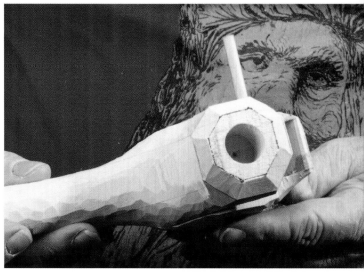

Progress.

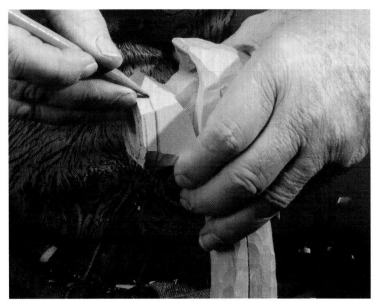

I'm reinforcing the line where the feathers will stop; this is also where I will begin angling the wood in toward the octagon mark.

Fit the handle on the spindle from time to time to make sure it still fits properly and you're on the right track.

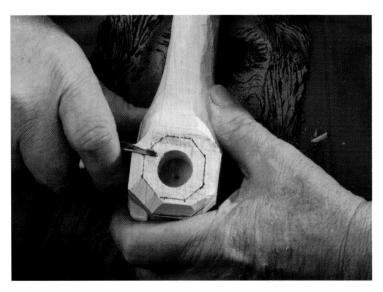

Make sure you don't cut in past the octagon mark.

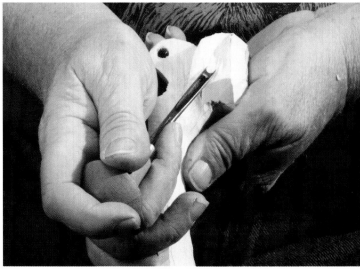

I'm using a #9 half-round gouge to narrow the neck a little bit. The gouge marks can also represent the feather texture, so if you make them in the right direction, you can save yourself some time in going back over the piece to add texture.

Progress.

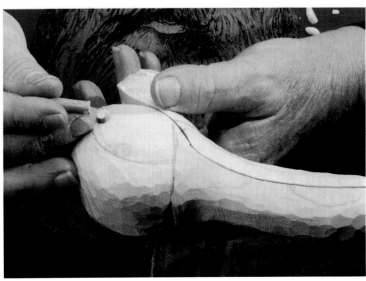

The excess on the dowel pin is getting in my way, so I'm cutting it off. Don't worry about cutting it so it's flush against the head just yet.

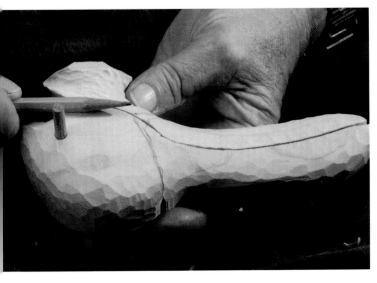

Now I'm marking where the beak will start. Measure (using your pencil) on both sides so that it is even on both sides. Draw a line all the way around.

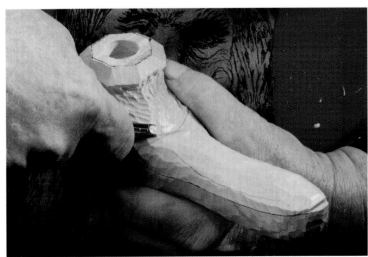

Now that the beak has been marked, I'm going to use the gouge again to bring the feather texture right up to the line.

Mark lines for the eyes like this. Check both sides against each other to make sure they are even.

Progress.

Use a V-tool to follow the beak line all around to define it a little more clearly.

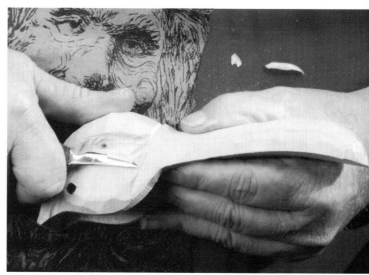

Use the knife to smooth out the roughness. Work around the cheekbone.

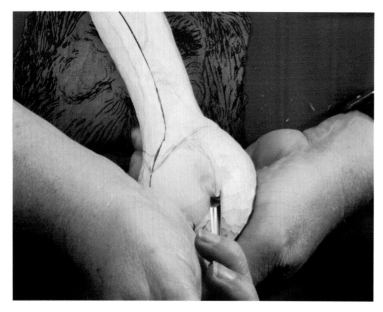

Now that the beak has been defined, I'm going to work on the eyeline. That will also define the cheekbone.

I'm using the V-tool to define the top of the head a little more.

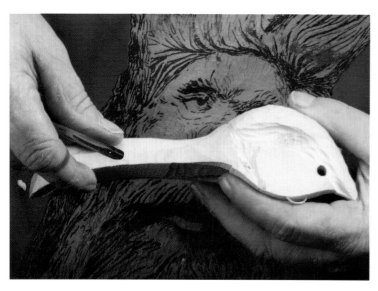

Progress. That knot looks like we could use it for the eye, but it's actually too far back.

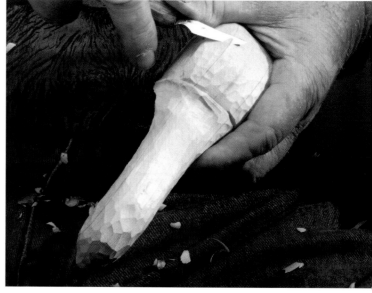

Now I'm going over the whole handle with the knife to get rid of any little lumps, knots, or sharp edges that shouldn't be there.

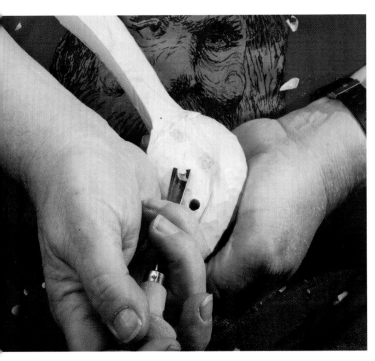

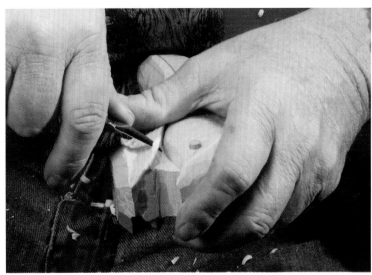

This area on the jaw piece near the hinge juts out a little too far, so I'm cutting it down.

The flat gouge can also add texture as you smooth the piece out.

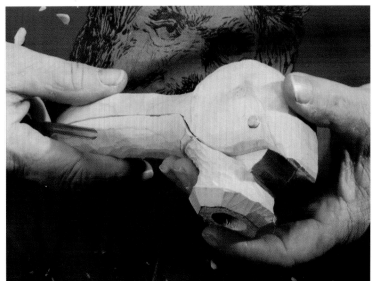

Progress.

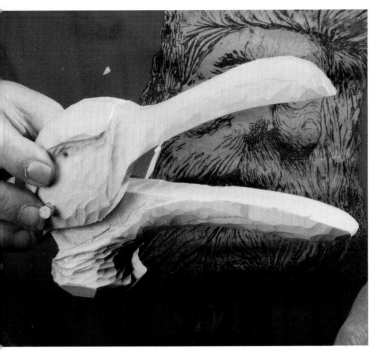

Progress. Fit the pieces back together with the dowel pin to make sure everything still lines up.

Now I'm going back with the half round gouge to put the feathery marks back.

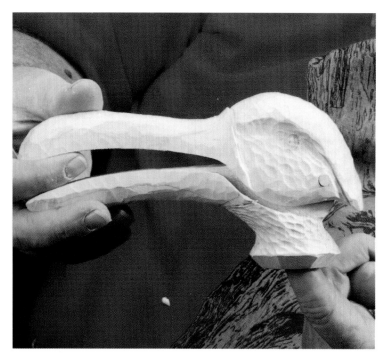

Progress.

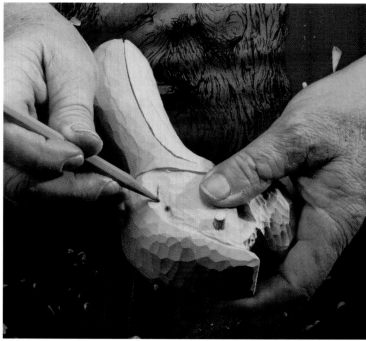

Now we will mark where the eyes belong.

Put it back on the spindle to check its alignment.

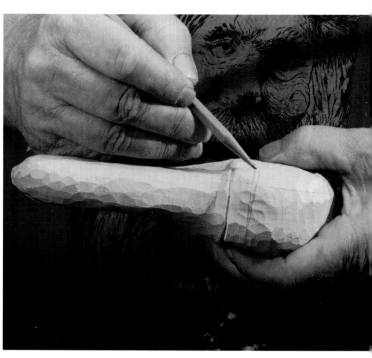

Mark both sides, making sure they're even. A good way to check is by drawing a line over the head from eye to eye.

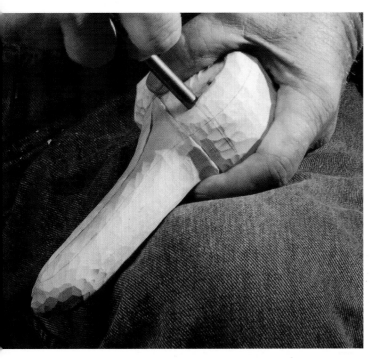

I'm using an eye punch to establish the eyeball right over the mark I've made. These are eye punches I have designed, and they are available exclusively through Woodcraft.

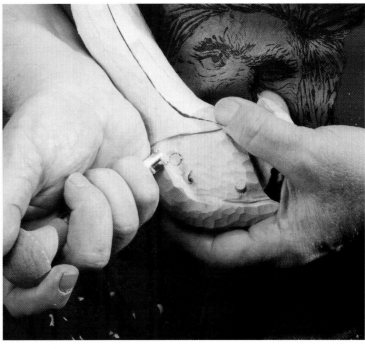

Use the gouge to shave off any pencil marks left. The sooner you do this, the better—the longer the pencil stays on, the more it smudges, and the dirtier the piece gets.

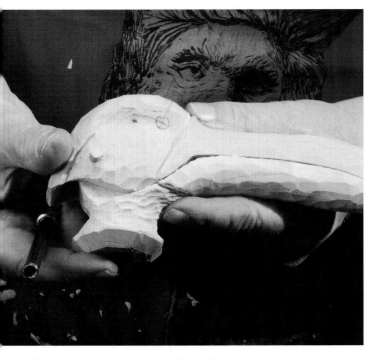

Here's the mark the eyepunch made.

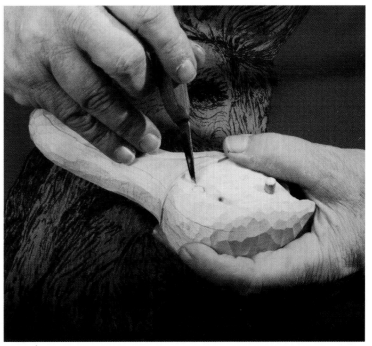

Three little cuts make a triangle to form the tear duct.

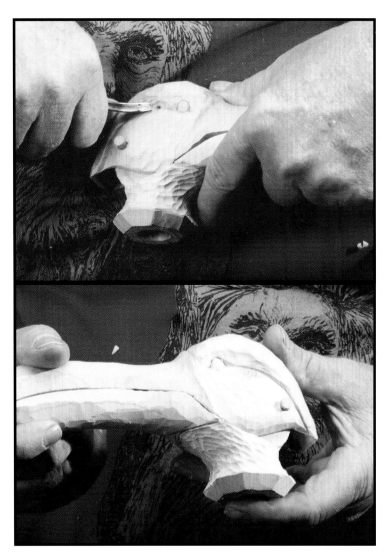

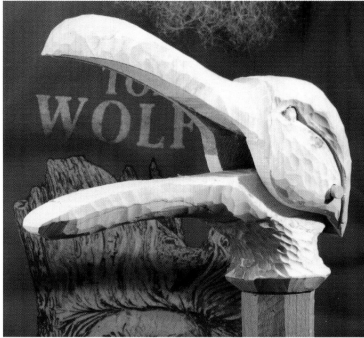

Progress.

The eye line should run the whole way down the hood.

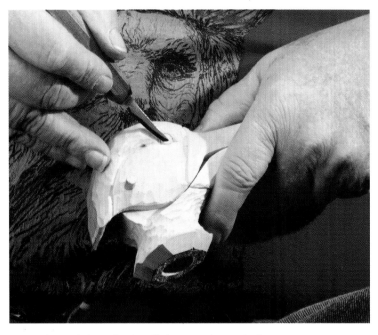

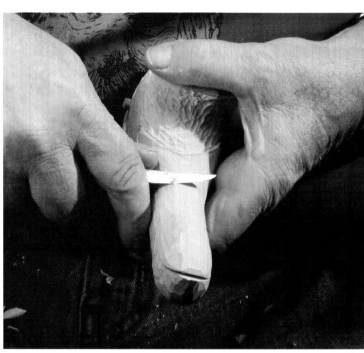

A good sharp knife will clean up the eyeball.

Look for any continuous carving lines you've made and break them up. Make sure you get rid of all saw marks, because when you paint the piece the saw marks will show up a different color.

24

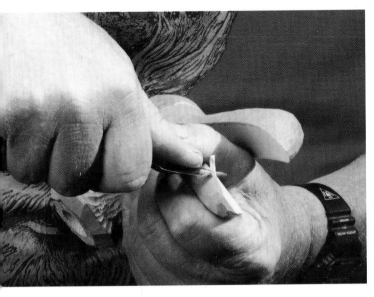

I'm carving off a little bit of the sharp edge of the bill to create a more natural-looking bevel.

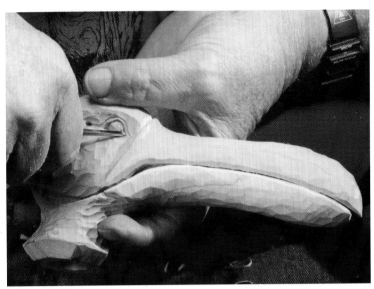

Then define the lower eyelid, also by starting in the center and moving out in each direction.

Progress.

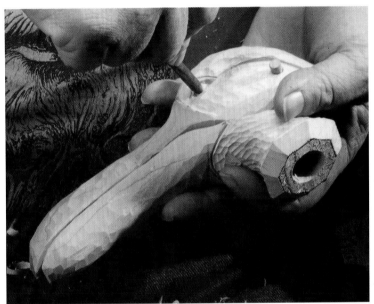

A smaller *eye* punch will define the pupil. I'm putting it a little more forward, but you can add it any way you like to get different expressions.

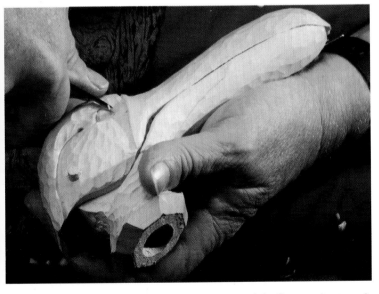

A small veiner or V-tool will define the eyelids. Start at the top of the eye and move down once in each direction.

The finished eye.

25

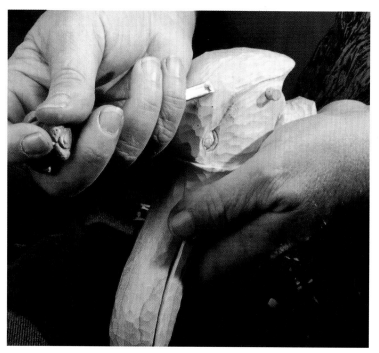

Now I'm going back with the half round gouge to refine the feather texture. There are wider feathers on the back of the head, and they get smaller as you move toward the bill. You can get as detailed as you like, but I'm keeping it simple for more of a folk art look.

The finished texture work. Now I'll sand it a little and it will be ready for painting.

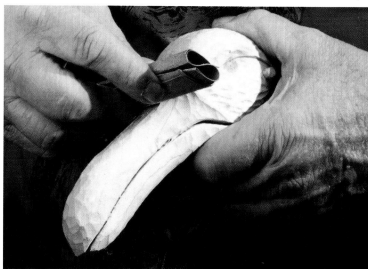

I like to fold the sand paper like this to sand with a rounded edge.

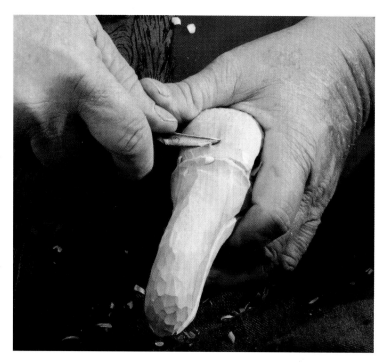

I'm going to let the feather texture fade out altogether closer to the face and finish it out with knife cuts.

Sand the bill as smooth as possible, eliminating all knife marks.

Progress.

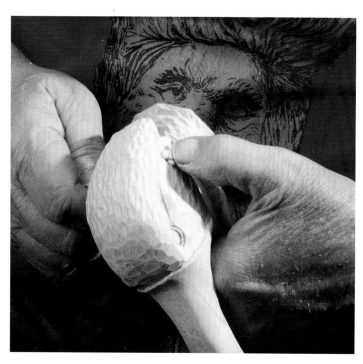

Now is the time to glue the pin in place. I like to use Elmer's. Glue it only on one side where the pin sticks out, and push it in so it's even with the side of the face.

Cut off any excess dowel that's poking out the other side so it also blends in with the side of the face.

Now we're ready to paint!

 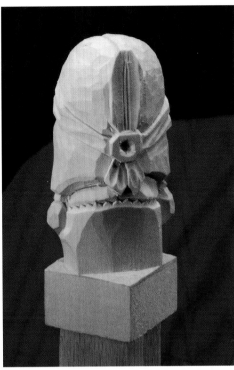 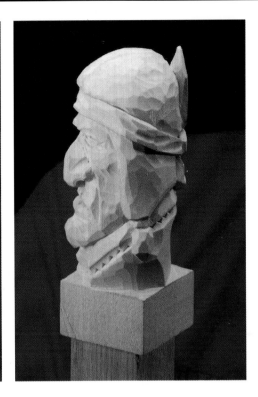

Of course, you can also carve a handle out of a single piece of wood. The process is similar to the bird we just carved, using the same steps for starting the piece and attaching it when it's finished.

This one attaches with a screw.

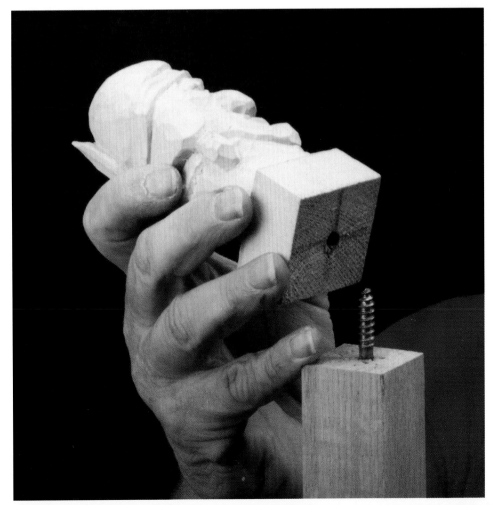

Painting and Finishing the Project

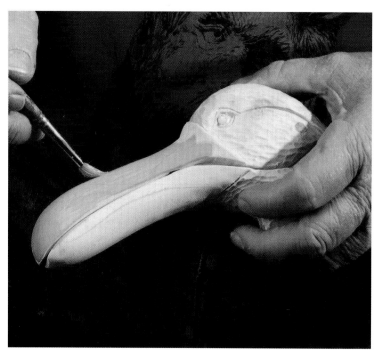

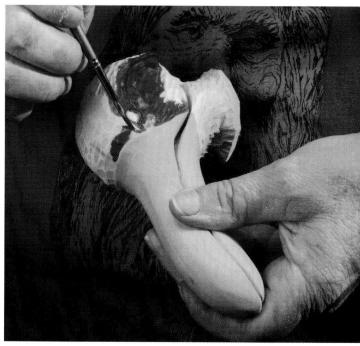

I like to paint with artist oil paints, thinned with turpentine into a stain. It lets the wood show through the paint. I'll start by painting the bill yellow.

The head of this bird will be a bright red—Alizarin Crimson, to be exact. Make sure you avoid the eye; we'll paint that in a minute.

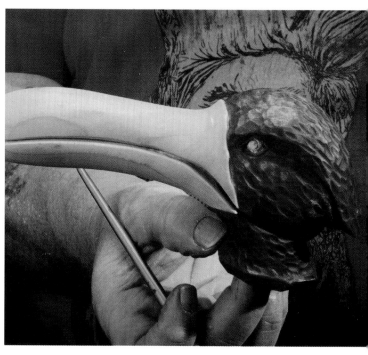

The bill. Blot away any extra paint with a paper towel.

It's a red-headed pecan cracker!

We'll keep using the bright colors and paint the inside of the bill vermillion.

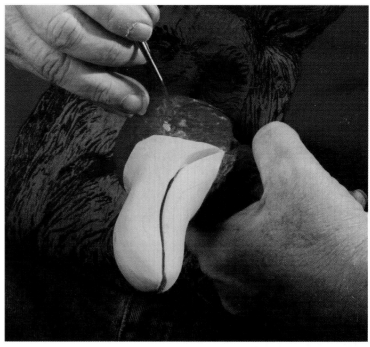

I'm adding a little vermillion around the outside of the eye to make it stand out more.

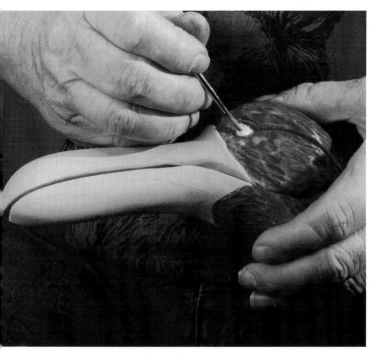

We'll give him blue eyes.

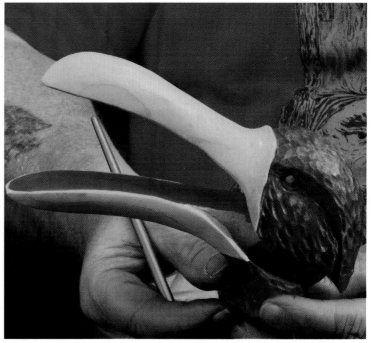

Progress.

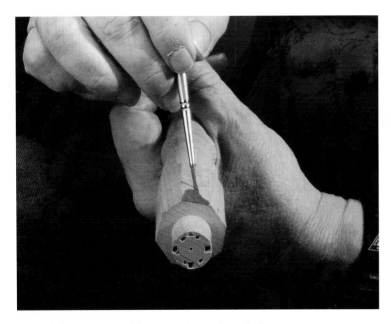

I also want to add some color to the spindle.

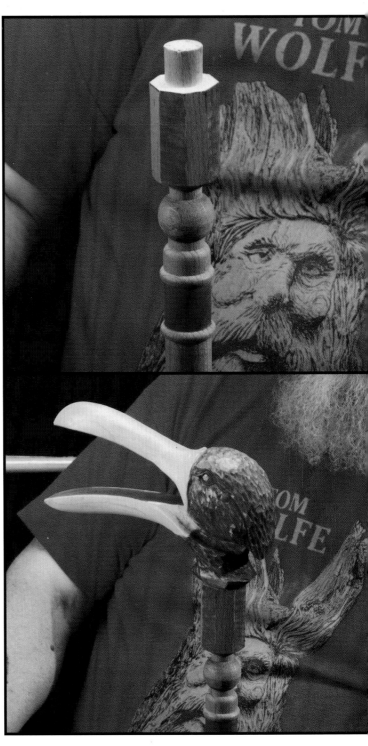

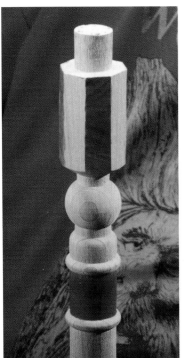

Progress.

Progress.

A little Deft semi-gloss spray on the spindle will dry the paint faster and make a nice gloss. Put the handle back on the spindle and spray that too.

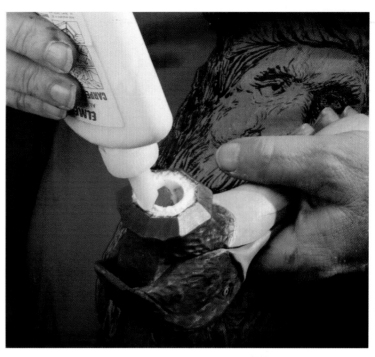

After you've sprayed the handle, add a tiny dot of black in the eye to create the pupil.

Now we can glue the handle onto the spindle. Elmer's works well. Make sure you use enough glue to make a strong bond, but you don't want it running down the cane. Let it sit overnight to let it dry completely.

Now spray the entire cane and let it dry overnight. You might want to smooth out any rough areas with steel wool and then add a second coat.

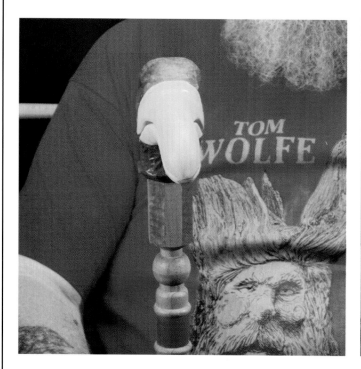
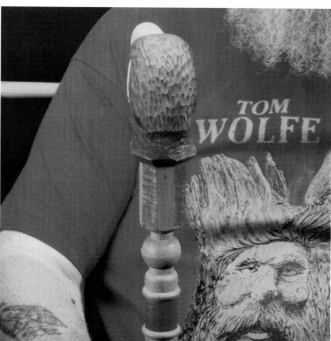

The finished cane.

Gallery

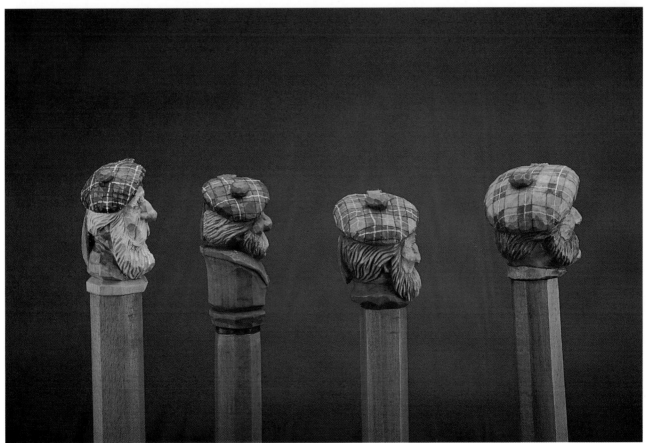